this book belongs to

. . . .

created by
micky book

copyright©2021

All rights reserved. No part of this book maybe reproduced, distributed, or transmitted in any form or by any means.

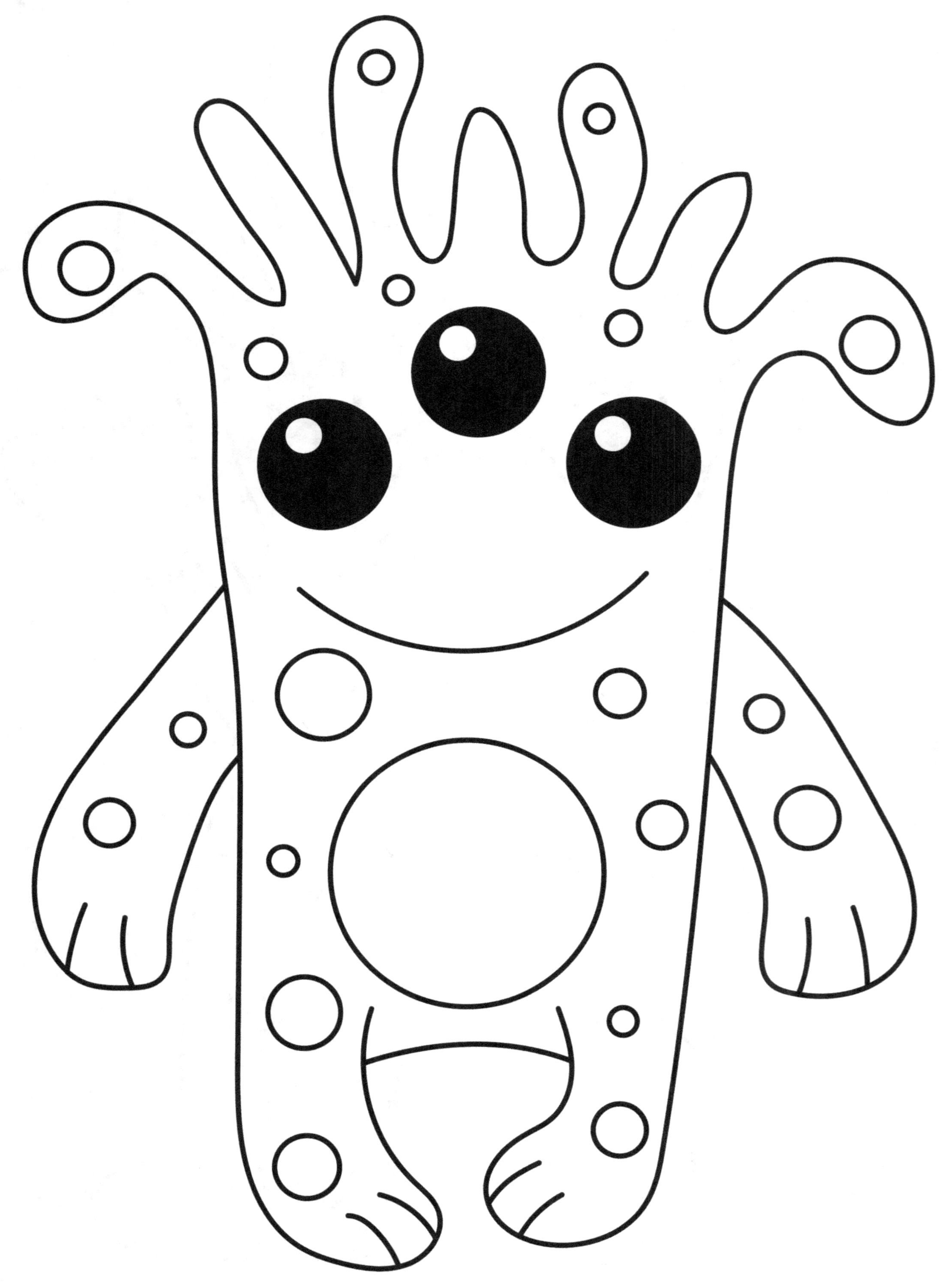

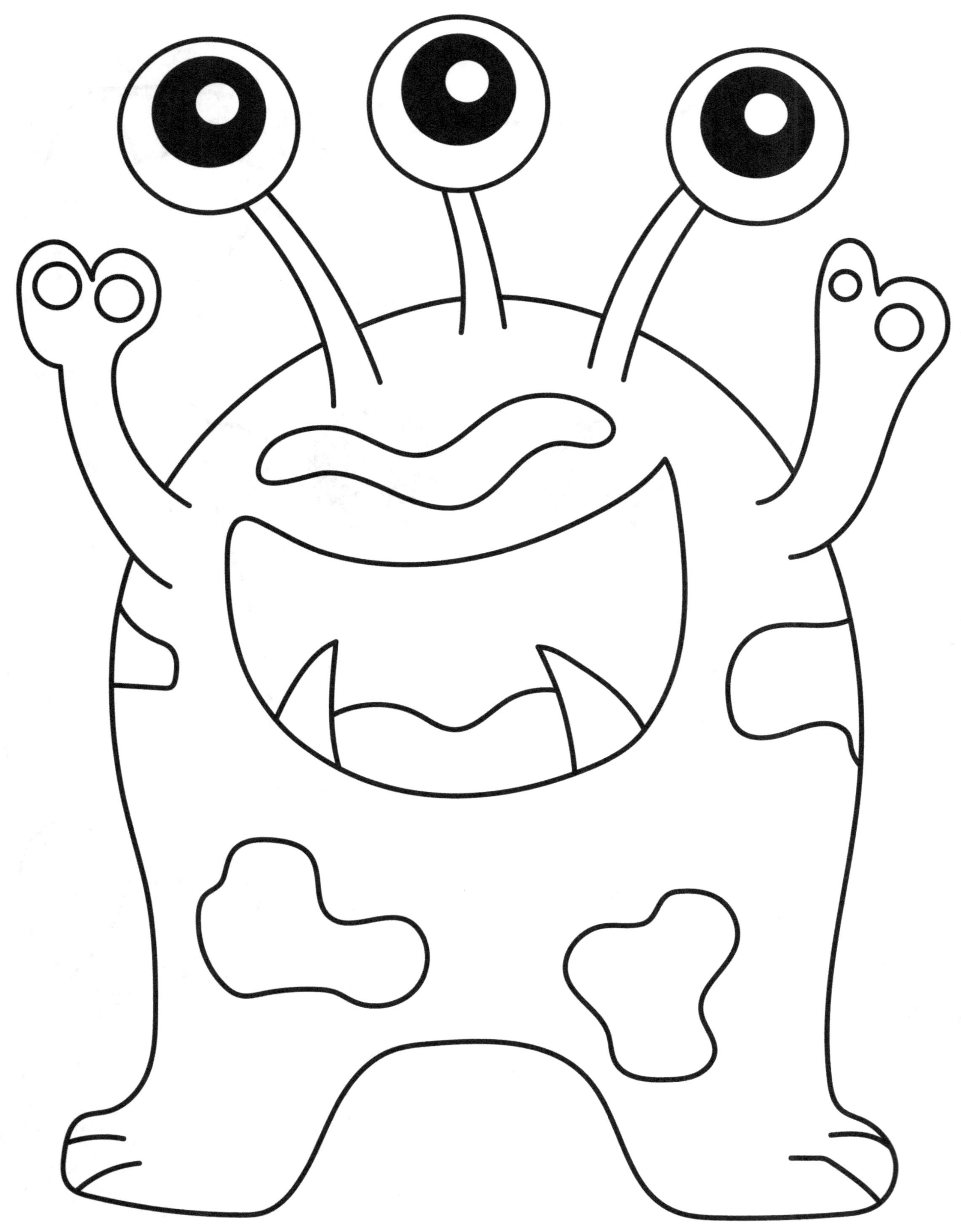

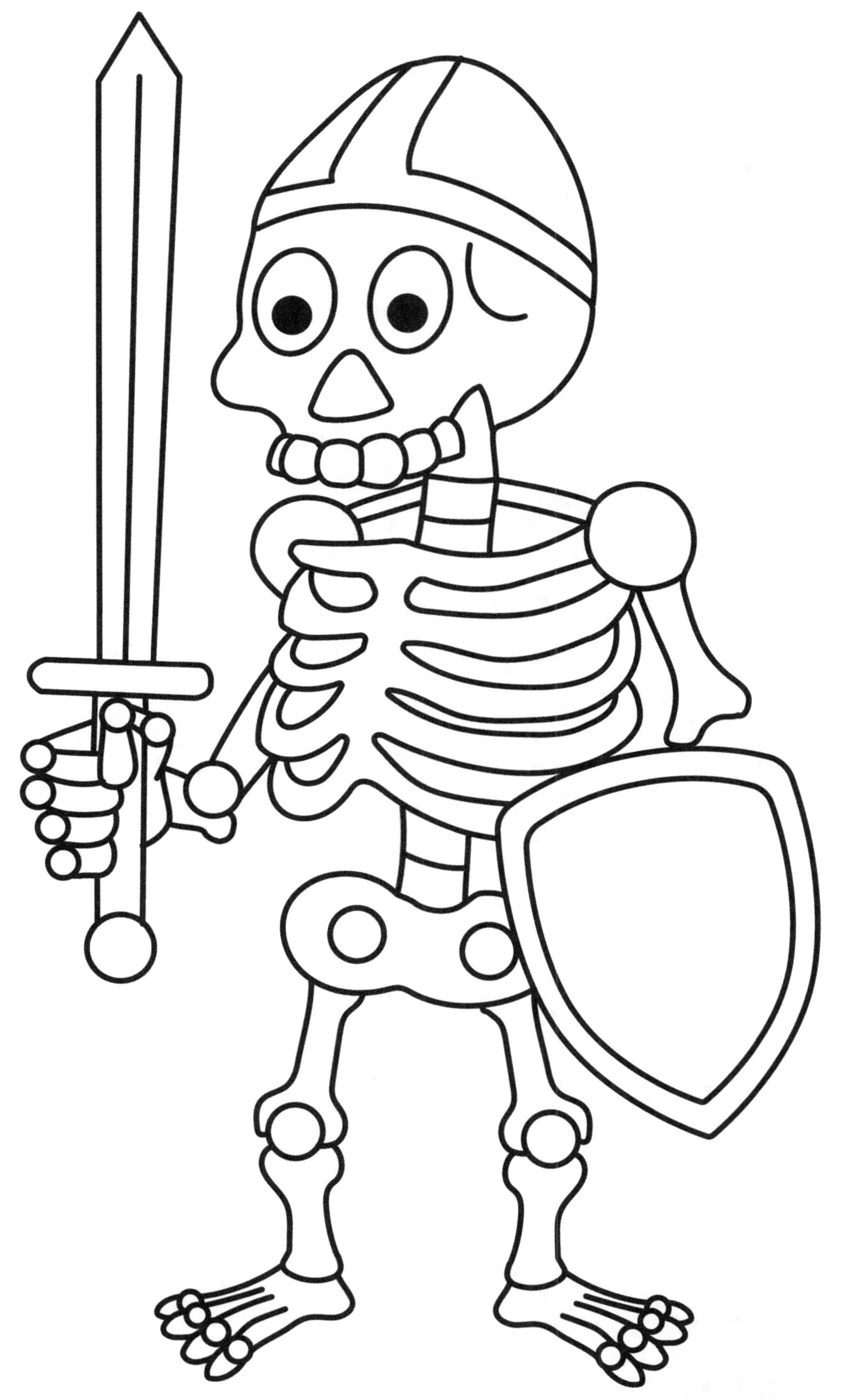

www.ingramcontent.com/pod-product-compliance
Lightning Source LLC
Chambersburg PA
CBHW081236250726
48654CB00012B/1343